iMAGE is POWER

Manage Your Mood; Improve Your Image; Create More Wealth

◀◀◀◀▶▶▶▶

Mic Alexander

AuthorHouse™
1663 Liberty Drive
Bloomington, IN 47403
www.authorhouse.com
Phone: 1-800-839-8640

© 2010 Mic Alexander. All rights reserved.

No part of this book may be reproduced, stored in a retrieval system, or transmitted by any means without the written permission of the author.

First published by AuthorHouse 1/11/2010

ISBN: 978-1-4490-4906-5 (e)
ISBN: 978-1-4490-4904-1 (sc)
ISBN: 978-1-4490-4905-8 (hc)

Library of Congress Control Number: 2009913658

Printed in the United States of America
Bloomington, Indiana

This book is printed on acid-free paper.

Cover Artwork by: Martin Peterson
Photos by: Charles Couch
Editor: Denise Lasley

The author and those associated with this book do not dispense medical advice nor prescribe the use of any technique discussed in this book as a form of treatment for physical, medical or emotional problems without the advice of a physician. The intent of this book is to offer information. IN the event you use any of the information in this book for yourself, which is your constitutional right, the author and those associated with this book assume no responsibility for your actions.

Quoted portions or material otherwise attributed appears with permission or relates to matter of communication within the public domain. Every effort has been made to secure prior authorization, and any non-compliance is purely inadvertent.

Dedication

This book is dedicated to my parents Marie and Elmore Alexander. It would take a novel to thank you for all you have done – and still do – to shape my life. There are many people who feel that they have the best parents in the world; when I observe family relationships around me, I KNOW that I do. I cherish your willingness to be processed and to continue learning at a season in your lives when you could refuse to grow anymore and simply "ride the wave" into the sunset. Your vibrancy, wisdom and vitality are an inspiration to all who know you. I thank God for every moment I am allowed to be present with you on this journey.

TABLE OF CONTENTS

◀◀◀◀▶▶▶▶

Dedication	v
About this book	x
Introduction	xiii
Chapter 1. Study	1
Chapter 2. iMAGE	7
Chapter 3. You	15
Chapter 4. Processing	25
Chapter 5. Moods	33
Chapter 6. Games	51
Chapter 7. What games are you playing?	59
Chapter 8. Ethics	75
Conclusion	83
Acknowledgements	85
About the Author	90

*The **image** of myself which I try to create in my own mind in order that I may love myself, is very different from the **image** which I try to create in the minds of others in order that they may love me.*

W. H. Auden

About this book

The labor of giving birth is very comparable to the labor of giving birth to one's dreams. There is great pain. We can experience it as an endurable moment because we know that the dream is being born. But if we think our dream is dying, then the same pain becomes unbearable. Mood management is the difference that matters in how we perceive, process and experience the moment.

If you are getting what you want in all areas of your life, this is not the book for you. If, however, there is something you always wanted to do, be, have or see and for whatever reason(s) you have not yet manifested your desires; or if you find yourself immobilized by fear, anger, boredom, depression and are unable to direct your energy to take action and get results, then read on. But before you do, there is something you must understand. To achieve the results that have, until now, eluded you, what is required is a willingness to "expand your box", to forego judgment about the material provided, to study and then to use your will to take action. Understand that these requirements are not easy. If they were, you would already be doing, being, having and seeing what you want in your "presence" time.

By the end of our time together, you will have a better understanding of concepts that are probably already familiar to you. If you apply them, you will build a powerful image and receive the following benefits:

- *Increased Self-Awareness and the ability to manage your moods*
- *Increased Ability to Manage Stress*
- *Increased Presence – Concentration and Focus*
- *Increased Ability to Study and Learn*
- *Increased Ability to Handle People with Grace and Confidence*
- *Increased Ability to Lead and Be Led*
- *Increased Ability to Have More Fun, Be Friendlier and Attract More Friends*
- *Increased Enthusiasm For Life and More Optimism About the Future*

These increased abilities help build an iMAGE that empowers you to take action and create the results you want in your personal and professional life….because iMAGE is Power.

Keep Going … Keep Growing

INTRODUCTION

My primary identity is Mic Alexander. Professionally, I have had the pleasure of playing many games: formal education, banking, insurance, real estate and telecommunications to name a few. I have experienced many wins playing entrepreneurial games in the arenas of multilevel marketing, make up, import clothing, and custom jewelry. But my greatest challenges and most valuable lessons came from the commercial printing game.

My role as CEO of my family's commercial printing company for 17 years exposed me to a playground of competition, fans, opponents, rules, regulations, limitations, liberties, losses and wins. Things were going well. Fourteen years into the game, my parents were able to retire and I quickly discovered the difference between my abilities and my skills.

I became so good at the game that I was asked to serve as a member of several boards and also received many honors and awards including the *Chamber's Entrepreneur of the Year, Largest Minority Business* and *People of Prominence Award*. It wasn't until the "end of game" that I was forced to confront the real cause of my success. Said another way, it wasn't until I "lost" that I discovered my wins.

By now you have realized that the language I am using is comprised of familiar words used in an unfamiliar context. This is the language of the **iMAGE Wealth Management** technology (**iWM**). It is designed to trigger the brain and reorganize old ideas that may or may not be supporting us in achieving results. Read on! In time, you will become very comfortable hearing and articulating this new and powerful language.

The business climate changed first. The people with whom I played my game began playing different games. Some of them were promoted, demoted, replaced or won over by my opponents. Then the industry changed. Consumers began printing in-house and printing equipment tripled in cost as digital technology emerged. The crushing blow was the unexpected loss of our largest client and the downturn in the economy in 2008.

I was fortunate to have **Green Zone** timing (being in the right place at the right time and with the right people). Our company's high standard of ethics over the years earned me relationships with experts in the fields of business transition, financial management and legal policies. These contacts "volunteered" to guide us through the turbulent waters of "end of game". I was able to sell the company's assets, clear our debt, retain our preferred credit status and earn a profit, which positioned me to play the next game.

So now, you might be wondering, *"Well, what was the loss?"* The fact that the game ended prematurely was more than a major upset for me … it was a shock. What I hadn't realized was that over the 17 years at the helm of the company I came to believe that *I was* my company. My identity as Mic Alexander, CEO, successful business owner, Entrepreneur of the Year and employer, had taken over all aspects of my life. Since I was not married and had neither children nor pets, (I'm telling you that I was totally dedicated to this role/identity), I was shocked and devastated when the role suddenly vanished. It didn't help when I ran into people who would say "Hey, aren't you the president of that printing company?" Adding insult to injury was the sudden disappearance of all those who I thought were my friends; the people who hugged on me at the "network" meetings, played golf with me and invited me to go boating. I was forced to face the fact that it was just business and nothing more. I found myself in the blackness – nowhere – not here. I became absent.

Through the seven month period following the "end of game", I experienced a wide range of moods. Some moods lasted hours, some days, but they transitioned in this order: *chaos, betrayal, remorse, failure, fear, panic, rage, boredom, centered, trusting, persistence, strength, relieved, cheerful, focused, optimistic, creative, positive, action.*

Study the moods again. The order in which they occurred is of vital importance. Each mood was trending upward rather than downward. I allowed myself to fully experience each mood. When I say, "I allowed myself to experience each mood," I mean that I resisted the urge to suppress my "negative" e-motions and gave myself permission to feel them, placing a time limit of 2 days on the worse ones. The result was that I began to naturally progress to the next mood without effort. I came to realize that this is the natural order when moving through life experiences. This is why mood management is one of the four important steps in developing a wealthy iMAGE.

I don't have all the answers. But I have learned a technique that works. I survived the shock of my situation and emerged winning, friendly and empowered to play my next game. Not everyone can say the same. Some people get stuck in depression, anger and victimhood. Some choose to end all games – period. I however, discovered my *Super Being-ness* at a time when my mind and body were exhausted to the point of surrender. I raised my mood level, re-aligned my thoughts, refined my skills through study and practice, re-accessed my iMAGE and took action over my new game. My intention is to help individuals and organizations experience the same winning results using the iMAGE Wealth Management technology.

STUDY ▸▸▸

Studying may well be the single greatest reason we fail to create results in our lives. Most adults, even those who have participated in higher education, have never fully learned -- or have forgotten -- how to study.

Somewhere in the midst of our experiences, beliefs, precepts and judgments are the facts about a topic. The ability to correctly observe and perceive the who, whats, whens, whys and hows of a situation is an ability that most adults have failed to refine. Once you become more present in an area by increasing your knowledge through the art of study while maintaining a high mood level, you will unlock your power to create the life you want, whenever you want, with freedom and ease.

☐ Yes ☐ No Do you own a dictionary?
☐ Yes ☐ No Do you know where it is?
☐ Yes ☐ No Have you used it in the past 7 days?

Don't be embarrassed if your answer to any of these questions is no.

It simply means that you have not experienced the effectiveness of the dictionary and the power of words when creating results in your life.

To master this topic (or any topic), you will need a good dictionary. I recommend the *American Heritage Dictionary* or *Webster's Dictionary of the English Language.* Although I often use the on-line dictionary services, I find that holding a book in my hand and feeling the pages has a greater and more lasting impact upon my studies. Spoken as a former player of a rapidly changing industry (printing), there is no substitute for paper!

Researching words in the dictionary, especially the most commonly used words is the first step to reclaiming your power that may have been decreased through multiple upsets and shocks along your journey. Mispronounced, misused and/or misspelled words indicate that further study is in order.

*Reclaim your power
by researching the definition of words for yourself
rather than using someone else's projected definition
that you have accepted as true.*

You will notice that I have condensed many of the definitions used in this system. I believe that one of my gifts is to make complicated things simple and summarizing the definitions is my way of helping you to have a more precise but accurate definition to work with. But please, research the words yourself before accepting my definitions.

I also strongly recommend reading aloud whenever you are in study mode. Reading aloud forces you to concentrate on each word you read. As you read aloud take note of any physical manifestations such as stuttering or mispronouncing words. This may be an indication that those words need further defining. Don't let your ego fool you. If you notice any of these signs, take a moment to look up the word, no matter how simple or common.

I invite you to use your dictionary to study the definitions on the pages that follow. Don't be afraid to challenge what you are reading. Research the words and find a definition that you can agree with. When you can get a 3D definition of a word, that is -- an accurate definition plus a picture in your mind -- you will feel the power of that knowledge in the form of confidence when using the word.

For example, if I say the word *car* to you, you will most likely have an accurate definition of the word: *a vehicle used for travel*, and a picture will pop up into your mind. It might be a picture of the vehicle you currently own or one that you dream of owning, but I am certain that some picture will appear.

If, however, I say the word *celiograph* to you, your mind and body will go through a series of short circuits trying to access the correct data. You will notice several physical manifestations that alert you that further research of the word is needed, such as blinking or rolling eyes, frown or smile, hands to temples, or even yawning. Pay attention. Don't let your ego rob you of your power! Take time to look up the words that you may need to further define, no matter how small or familiar the word may seem. I guarantee that you will experience a real sense of excitement as you improve your vocabulary, your spelling skills and reclaim your personal power.

By using a dictionary you will move from awareness to understanding to knowing or knowledge. And knowledge is power.

By the way, don't bother researching *celiograph*. I made it up!

Note to Students:

At the end of each chapter I have allotted space to record your thoughts and definitions. Thoughts may surface as you read the material. They may be in the form of questions, strong disagreement or "Ah-ha" moments. Record them in the space provided then review them after completing the book. You may notice a shift in your precepts, beliefs, or personal power. Use the space provided marked "definitions" to expand your knowledge of words. Challenge yourself to review a minimum of one word per chapter. You will be amazed at what you might learn about words you frequently use. Over time, your dictionary will become as important to you as your identification – you won't want to leave home without it.

Thoughts...

Definitions...

iMAGE ▸▸▸

When I initially began working on iMAGE Wealth Management in 2006, the system was called Image Risk Management. The word *risk* created an immediate **Red Zone mood** for some people, making them resistant to the concept. (It was funny to see that those resistant to the word *risk* were the very people that had the biggest risk to either their personal or professional image.)

iWM was born out of a desperate need to manage my printing company's image in the marketplace as we expanded our employees, vendors and client base. When the company consisted of just my Dad, Mom and I, it was easy to control what others perceived about our company and product because we all believed in the same code of ethics.

**The greatest risk to any company image
is its employees,
especially those who come in direct contact
with clients or the public.**

Employees who are unhappy, untrained or uninformed can project a poor self-image, which reflects on the company as a whole.

My solution to the growing problem of managing my company's image was a system I created called **THE SHOW . . . *Because you are always on*.** The scoring system measures image risks in five specific areas of business.

I also created a version called **THE PRIVATE SHOW,** which measures an individual's image in the same five areas.

1. The ***Home Show*** evaluates your customers' experiences when they visit your facility (The Private show for individuals measures the experience of anyone visiting your home or office).
2. The ***Talk Show*** evaluates your customers' experiences when coming in contact with your communications, whether written, verbal or automated (same for individuals).
3. The ***Stage Show*** evaluates your customers' experiences when coming in direct contact with your product or service (for individuals: evaluates their roles/identities and vision).
4. The ***Road Show*** evaluates your customers' experiences when coming in contact with your sales staff and/or sales materials (for individuals: outward appearance and vocabulary).
5. The ***Trade Show*** evaluates your customers' experiences when transacting business (for individuals: code of ethics).

Today, **THE SHOW** is being used by companies and individuals to mitigate the damages associated with risks to their image.

While developing **THE SHOW**, I became totally immersed in the topic of image. What is it and what role does it play in our successes and failures? Here is what I came to understand.

> **Image** can be defined as the sum total of all that is believed about an individual, product or business/organization. Although it may not be accurate or factual, in our society, perception is reality.

The iMAGE you project may not always be an accurate reflection of who *YOU* really are.

Perhaps you just found out that someone close to you is filing bankruptcy, their home is in foreclosure and they may need to come live with you and your family until they can regroup. You're sitting at your desk at work feeling powerless and frustrated. A co-worker, who also happens to be a friend, interrupts you and without looking up you ask, *"What the h---- is it now?"*

When you do look up, you notice this person is standing there waiting to introduce you to the new manager. Now you will spend the first courting hours of your relationship with your new boss trying to undo that first impression. Yikes!!! It's not really who you are! It was just one moment in time.

When you know who *YOU* are and can manage your iMAGE, you will improve your communication skills, handle people with finesse – regardless of your mood level and theirs, find yourself in the right places at the right times with the right people, and attract abundance in all the areas of your life that you desire.

I am well aware that the outside image you project is extremely powerful. I have consulted with many people on their wardrobe, hairstyle, choice of eyewear, etc. However, I believe that if you are projecting a powerful image from the inside, you can more easily overcome what people judge about you from the outside because iMAGE is Power!

> **Wealth** can be defined as an abundance of any-thing YOU desire.

The most common definition of wealth is perceived to be: a great quantity or store of money, valuable possessions, property, or other extravagant riches. But real wealth is not limited to things. *Wealth can be an abundance of time, health, love, laughter and more.*

Many people have asked me to explain the difference between wealth and prosperity. Of course, I tell them to look both words up in the dictionary. My personal understanding is that *wealth* is an abundance of anything you desire and *prosperity* is the condition of enjoying that abundance. This explains why some very wealthy people are also very miserable. They are lacking prosperity.

One of the most important exercises that anyone can do to help create the life they desire is to define their personal perception of wealth. I have found that it is different things to different people. It may very well be financial abundance, but what else is it? Ask yourself to define wealth in terms of things that money cannot buy. Don't overlook things like sunshine, rain, and clean air. These are things that many of us take for granted. However, if we didn't have them, all the money in the world couldn't stop our eventual demise.

image

Wealth . . . what is it to YOU?

_____
_____
_____
_____
_____
_____
_____
_____
_____
_____

Need help? The chart on the following page lists some of the answers my students have described as wealth (in no particular order, but I have taken the liberty to combine some of them. My additions are in bold.). Check off the ones that you can accept as a part of your definition.

	Quality time with children/grands	Harmony in personal relationships
	Rain/forest, thunder, storms	Laughter/Crying to release
	Sun rise/set, shinny days	Sharing/Giving
	A garden that bares fruit	Clean running water/ Hot Shower
	Good Food/Great wine/Great Friends	Shoes that don't hurt
	Parents/Grands being alive and well	A relationship with God
	The time to draw (create)/all art forms	Effective communication
	Clean air	Kind neighbors
	Job/enjoyable/purposeful	Learning/**STUDYING**
	A good relationship with siblings	Being an aunt/uncle
	No major illnesses/ Healthy body	The use of all 5 senses/ all limbs
	Wisdom/Intuition/The "little voice"	Teaching
	Loving foster parents/ Foster children	Cooking
	The Ocean/sports & activities associated)	The Sun/Moon/Stars/4 Seasons
	Air conditioning/ Electricity	Access to Health Care
	Fellowship and Socializing	A loving church home/spiritual comm.
	Clothing	Plays/Operas/Movies
	Volunteering/Special Olympics & others	Hanging out with active seniors
	Help when needed	**MOOD MANAGEMENT** Techniques
	A POSITIVE IMAGE	**POWER**
	A CLEAR VISION	**ENTHUSIASM**

iMAGE Wealth Management (iWM) *is a system that focuses on utilizing an **i**ndividual's **M**oods, **A**bilities, **G**ames & **E**thics to control and "make more of" what others perceive while attracting wealth.*

No matter what game you are playing in life (relationship, business, social, academic, health, sports, etc.), your ability or skill in the area combined with your mood and ethics creates the iMAGE to which others are either attracted or repelled.

iMAGE Wealth Management begins with YOU, the individual. It is a system that teaches YOU how to manage your mood, identify your abilities vs. skill, develop a "game" plan and review your code of ethics. Once your iMAGE is established you can set an intention to use it to create wealth. When YOU can perceive that YOU want something, set an intention to get it, formulate a plan of action and have the power to implement the plan, ***the result is wealth - an abundance of anything you desire.***

iMAGE is POWER

Thoughts . . .

Definitions . . .

You ▸▸▸

To get results from the iWM technology, one must have a thorough understanding of several definitions.

What is your definition of YOU?
If all of your roles and identities were suddenly removed, who would YOU then be?

Don't be embarrassed if you find yourself without a definitive answer to this question. Most adults I informally interviewed answered this question using descriptive characteristics such as honest, ethical, loving, etc. Some of them described their roles or identities such as mom/dad, teacher, doctor, etc. And they all agreed that both characteristics and roles can change, so YOU must be something greater.

iWM supports the idea that YOU are not just your character, role, identity, mood, mind or body. YOU are the energy that has the ability to control all of the above. To successfully utilize this system in building wealth, it is necessary to thoroughly understand the difference between YOU, Mind, and Body.

> **YOU** can be thought of as the energy that connects your breath to your heart beat; your essence, the life force plus your experiences. Spirit.

The late Alan Walter, author of the book *The Secrets to Increasing Your Power, Wealth and Happiness,* describes YOU as an acronym for "Your Own Universe". I like his analogy because it is easily recognizable. For example, your home is a reflection of YOU. If you have an office or cubicle at work, it is more than likely adorned with items that represent your knowledge and mastery, such as diplomas and awards, as well as photos of family or friends, and other items that symbolize your viewpoints or pleasures. It is uniquely yours and has distinct differences from the other offices or cubicles. Your car, music collection, home, yard, foods in your refrigerator and cupboards, art, books, furniture, clothing, etc. are all part of your own universe and under your control. You can decide what stays, goes and changes. You can add and delete at any time YOU choose.

**It is important to realize that
YOU are in control of Your Own Universe
and although YOU may have some influence,
YOU are NOT in control of anyone else's.**

> ***Spirit*** *can be thought of as the nonmaterial characteristic of beings; the life force, the vital power, YOU.*

Many of us are familiar with the term "team spirit". We recognize that it is a non-physical energy that is comprised of each individual's image: their moods, abilities, the game and their code of ethics. Team spirit is the power that moves the team forward in space and time.

The same power exists in individuals. For example, it is easy for us to accept a newborn baby as a spiritual being. Without the skill to communicate its needs to us in words, it takes total command of our own universe by asserting its will in specific mood levels. Its spirit is so powerful that it can command the attention of anyone that crosses its path.

If you are playing the game of parenting, you will find yourself reacting to your baby's every mood. If she is crying, you will check her diaper or try rocking, a bottle, a pacifier, music or anything else your mind presents as a solution to the problem until you and your baby have a win. And how will you recognize a win? You will experience a happy, friendly, relaxed spiritual being that brings YOU joy just to be in its presence.

Let me address the subject that usually surfaces whenever I speak on YOUr spirit and that is the acknowledgement of a "higher source or power", the Holy Spirit, Jesus, God, Allah, Buddha, and a host of other names that are used to represent a universal intelligence greater than we as individuals. I am not the judge of someone else's choice to believe or not believe in a power greater than they are as an individual. My opinion is that whether you choose to believe that YOU walk the path alone or with a force or forces outside of YOU, this technology can be a benefit in creating results on your life journey. And I do believe that we are here to make more of not less of our time here.

> *Mind* can be described as an instrument used for recording past experiences and storing memories including pictures, feelings and data. It then uses this data to plan strategies that move the body and spirit forward in space and time while presenting solutions to obstacles that thwart those plans that are to be executed by the body.

There have been thousands of books written on just this topic alone. I will hardly attempt to cover the depth of all that is truth about the mind. My intention at this point is to help YOU understand that YOU are in control of the mind and not the reverse.

Do not underestimate the power of the mind
*to use its data to convince YOU
that the information it is presenting
is the absolute truth.
It may be the truth, but chances are,
it is simply reality and not the truth, "the whole truth".
It is important to know the difference.*

For example: "The earth is flat!" For centuries, this statement was believed to be the absolute truth, until ancient Greek philosophers challenged their own belief systems. The 5th century BC was considered to be the birth of consciousness, though it was not easy convincing people to let go of false beliefs. Some were so committed to their beliefs that they resorted to violence rather than "expand their box". Their minds convinced them that changing their reality would somehow be harmful to their life force and threaten their survival.

This is happening to each of us every minute of every day. The mind is constantly evaluating minor and major situations and providing several solutions that direct the body to protect our life force so that we may continue fully experiencing the physical world. The data used to compile these solutions are from many sources including past personal experiences, the experiences of others, various media sources and reading materials to name a few. Just beware that all solutions may not be feasible, or even logical, but once the solutions are presented, then YOU must make the choice of which to implement.

Not quite convinced? Here is another example. I had a leak in my basement. I/spirit observed that there was a leak and perceived that there was an urgent need to stop the water from seeping into the downstairs recreation room. My mind began searching its data banks for anything it has ever experienced, read or heard about flooding and began presenting me/spirit with possible solutions. With each solution, it also presented mental pictures and history of similar past experiences, including all emotions associated with those experiences. Which led to a *precept* (a rule of conduct or a belief which may or may not be the truth). Examples of a precept include: "The bed MUST be made everyday" or "Politicians can't be trusted".

After my mind presented several solutions, I had to decide which solution would best serve me. The solutions that came to me were as follows:

Proposed Solution	Data (history, past experience, moods)	Precept
Call the plumber	The last time I called the plumber, it cost me a fortune and he didn't even fix the problem.	Plumbers are expensive. Plumbers can't be trusted.
Use towels to soak up water	You only have "good" towels because you just cleaned the linen closets and discarded all worn or soiled towels. Your neighbor used her towels when her basement flooded and had to throw them away because the red clay left permanent stains.	"Good" towels are for guest. "Good" towels are too expensive to be use for this purpose. There is such a thing as "good" towels.
Use the wet/dry-vac	The wet/dry-vac worked well when there was flooding at work.	The wet/dry vac is easy to use.

In the end, I chose the wet/dry-vac. The mind engaged the body to complete the task and I got a winning result.

Subconsciously, we are aware that our spirit is superior to our mind and body. We prove this each time we make comments such as "I must be losing my mind" or, "My mind is telling me this or that".

Recognizing that YOU are more
than your mind and body
is an essential element in having power
to take action in your life.
It is the very first step
in the process of creating results.

> **Body** can be defined as a chemically fed, principal mass which houses a mind and spirit and is used for implementing the mind's commands for attaining the desired results of the spirit or YOU.

There are millions of books written about the science of the body and the importance of maintaining its health. My intention is to help you understand your body's role in creating wealth and it is simply this: "Your body is a perfect servant of your mind."

Before you begin questioning why I am not addressing the subject of appearance and its role in creating wealth, let me explain that I am of the belief that iMAGE begins from the inside out. How the body is adorned with clothing, jewelry, tattoos, hair or not, fat or not, and any other physical representation of an identity, is of little concern if YOU are not able to manage your moods, abilities, games or ethics.

If your body is not responding the way YOU want it to;
if it is displaying an addictive behavior,
has dis-ease,
or has a protective layer
of unwanted excess covering it (fat),
it is "all in your mind".

This is the reason it is so important to give the mind and body down time to rest and rejuvenate. It is also important to constantly clean the mind's "discs" by examining negative moods and releasing the intense feeling you get when you think about them, and then assess your beliefs/precepts to determine if they are useful in moving YOU closer to your goals.

"The mind is its own place, and in itself can make a Heaven of Hell, a Hell of Heaven."

John Milton

Thoughts . . .

iMAGE is POWER

Definitions . . .

PROCESSING ▸▸▸

> ***Processing:*** *The process of altering flawed or false beliefs to a more positive and empowering position through the use of specialized drills and questions. The result of processing often includes a rise in mood level, more enthusiasm, and an increase in personal power needed to attain results.*

Processing is a skill that is usually performed by a trained processor*. However, there are certain basic exercises that can be learned which help YOU begin to be more aware of negative data. When you properly handle this data, YOU will have more control over managing your mood when that subject resurfaces in your future, resulting in less stress.

---
* See Acknowledgements – Author Alan C. Walter

*When YOU can manage your mood
during challenging times,
the mind has more energy
to run its process of providing solutions
and YOU will have more power
to choose the best solution.
The body will have the energy
to carry out the necessary actions
resulting in a win, even in challenging times.*

Simple Process #1 - Presence:

Sit in a chair with both feet firmly on the floor, hands resting gently on your knees, eyes closed. For 90 seconds, name as many sounds as you can hear in your environment. Don't overlook outside noises such as airplanes, train horns in the distance, car engines, dogs barking, birds chirping, etc. Be fully present for 90 full seconds. Notice your breath, but do not force the natural rhythm to change. Feel the chair or sofa beneath you. Let your mind focus totally on the sounds YOU hear, and your breath. As you practice, try extending the time. Challenge yourself to sit for 10 minutes in this state without thought or judgment. Simply be present.

***Your ability to concentrate
and be fully present in*
*spirit, mind and body
is the first step to creating results.***

You wouldn't drive a racecar at 150 miles per hour and begin thinking about what you're going to eat for dinner. Because if you did, it would probably end up being your last super!

Presence is easier for some than others, but almost everyone has to practice to gain the skill of presence. A more advanced version of this process is to sit with another being, gazing eye to eye, in silence, each of you noticing your own breath and quieting your mind from thoughts or judgments. What sounds simple actually requires great skill. I strongly recommend that you begin by being present with nature and then refining your skill to include another spiritual being.

Once YOU are skilled at being fully present, you can begin noticing your communication to others and theirs to YOU while *Enhancing, Impairing, or Demolishing* people and/or situations (the EID process).

Our society has a tendency towards focusing on the negative, and we often impair or demolish others [their dreams, goals, ideas, spirits, etc.] without ever noticing. We do it to others and others do it to us. Pay attention to your mood and the words you use when speaking of others or about situations.

For example, when asked, *"How was your weekend?"* you might respond:

(Enhance) "It was quiet but I got a chance to catch up on my rest."

(Impair) "It was ok."

(Demolish) "Another boring weekend in this boring town."

Notice your mood and body language with each response. Even if it were "reality" that you experienced boredom over the weekend, YOU can keep your mood from dropping by enhancing or making more of the experience. *"I would have enjoyed being more active, so next weekend I will plan more activities."* Do you feel the power to take action in this response vs. the former? Don't freely give your power away. Take the high road – the **Green Zone** road.

Here is an example of the EID process as it relates to comments directed to YOU from another person. Sometimes the differences are very subtle.

(Enhance) "It's good to see you. You look really great!"

(Impair) "How are you? Are you still <u>trying</u> to work out?"

(Demolish) "You <u>shouldn't</u> be eating that. I heard about a new diet you might want to try."

When in person, observing another's physical manifestations and body language
can help you determine their real intention,
but it can also be heard in their tone.

If YOU feel someone is impairing or making less of you by running a "negative" process on you, your ability to manage their intention directly affects your mood. Your ability or skill to enhance their attempt to impair or demolish YOU is the key to creating a winning image. Judgment words such as "always", "never", "should", and "need to" are clear indications that an attempt to impair or demolish is in process.

For example, if someone comments: *"You should try this new diet I heard about,"* you might want to respond by saying:

"I Should? You don't think the cake and ice cream diet I'm using is working well for me?"

Oh, and don't forget to smile!

To be successful in this process YOU must be able to respond to your "negative processor(s)" with love and peacefulness, rather than harsh sarcasm or anger. There is great power in this process. However, to master it requires two very important things: one is to know who YOU are and the other is to practice. Once you become aware of this process and adopt it into your personal playing style, you will begin to notice it all the time. It is the same as purchasing a different make of car; you suddenly notice them everywhere as if the rest of the world decided to purchase it just because you did.

Simple Process #2 – EID Practice:

Listed next are a number of impairing/demolishing statements. Write an enhanced response for each. I have listed one possible solution for each statement after the exercise. Remember: *Practice makes perfect.*

1. "You never give me compliments."

_____
_____
_____

2. "What made you pick that shirt?"

_____
_____
_____

3. "…well, that's what you always do."

_____
_____
_____

4. "You really need to stop…"

_____
_____
_____

5. "You should be able to do that."

_____
_____
_____

Suggested Responses:

1. "You never give me compliments."

Never? I didn't realize that. But, thank you for calling it to my attention. I will attempt to be more inconsistent in the future.

2. "What made you pick that shirt?"

I don't know. At the time I thought it was a good choice. Do you like anything that I am wearing today?

3. "...well, that's what you always do."

Always? I didn't realize I was so disciplined. I am usually inconsistent when it comes to …

4. "You really need to stop…"

Thank you, but I really do have everything I need. However, I'm open to suggestions on ways to stop.

5. "You should be able to do that."

I should? I didn't realize the process of learning was so simple. Can you think of anything that might help me learn how, more quickly?

iMAGE is POWER

Thoughts . . .

Definitions . . .

Moods ▸▸▸

Okay, if you are still reading, I must be making a connection on some level...or at least arousing your curiosity. So, here is what we know so far:

- YOU are the life force, the energizer, the power, the perceiver of your want or need to create.
- YOU control the mind.
- Mind presents solutions intended to preserve your life force.
- YOU decide which solution is best.
- Mind directs the body to implement the solution.
- The body responds because it is a perfect servant of the mind.

Perhaps you are thinking, "If it's that simple, then why am I having difficulty getting the results I desire?" In order to achieve any result, YOU – your mind and body — must all be engaged simultaneously. If YOU perceive a want or need to create a result, the spirit is already on board.

For example:

"I want and need to go to the gym in the morning."

YOU are already onboard. When morning arrives the mind engages by saying, "Ok, YOU can do this. Let's go." But if the body sends a signal to the mind that indicates it is tired or injured, the result is incompletion.

Perhaps the body engages with full enthusiasm but the mind begins recounting reasons why the timing is not good: "We have a meeting at 9AM and there won't be enough time to workout and prepare." But if the spirit, mind and body are all in alignment and YOU are in a high mood level, the only possible outcome is completion – winning results.

iMAGE Wealth Management uses an individual's Moods, Abilities, Games and Ethics to create wealth – an abundance of anything you desire. Of these four, the one with the greatest impact on results is mood.

> **Mood** can be described as the emotional degree of intensity that one directs towards a certain outcome. Usually temporary, it is the state of mind or feeling resulting from one's perceived position or belief system. (Emotion by definition is a sensation or feeling for or against someone or something. E-motion = energy in motion. Example: If I toss a ball at you in the mood of happiness or playfulness, the energy is different than if I throw the ball at you in frustration or anger. E-motion can be thought of as the amount of effort it takes to cause a result.)

This is where the dictionary becomes most important. There are hundreds of moods. The average adult can describe only 10 to 15 of their own moods. The most common descriptions used are happy, excited, sad, hurt, afraid, angry, pissed, jealous, etc.

The first thing to remember is that YOU – the spiritual being – are NOT your mood. YOU are simply experiencing a specific mood at a specific time. YOU are in control of your ability to manage your mood and not the reverse. Saying, "I am angry," is much different than saying, "I am experiencing anger". The first phrase has a sense of permanency. The second phrase seems to imply your mood is temporary, allowing YOU to have more control over managing your anger.

In order to fully manage moods, one must be able to accurately identify the mood.

> *In order for YOU to be able to identify your mood, you must separate yourself from the mood. In essence, YOU must be bigger than your mood in order to describe it; otherwise, the mood is bigger than you.*

Think about that for a minute. Reread the statement. When any of my students question this statement I ask, "Could you accurately describe a person's hand if it is pressed against your face?"

Before I began studying mood management, my comfort mood was anger. No matter what "negative" (Red Zone) mood I was feeling, I would automatically classify it as anger. If I were disappointed in someone, I would react as if I were angry. Even if I were embarrassed, my mind would automatically send solutions responding to anger. It didn't take long for others to perceive me as a "hot head" or angry person – not the ideal iMAGE for an aspiring entrepreneur. My inability to manage my mood was negatively affecting my image, my relationships and ultimately my results.

When you are able to correctly perceive, observe and identify your own moods, you will increase your ability to detect the underlying moods of others. Spiritual beings are clever at masking their moods, but it is the underlying mood that is closer to the spiritual being's "reality" than the mood they may be projecting.

For example, the check out clerk in the grocery store may say hello with a slight smile, make brief eye contact with you, if at all, and then proceed to throw your food towards the bagging area. What do you think that being's mood really is?

Suppose you are working with a co-worker on a project and he projects moods of enthusiasm and confidence but when asked about his portion of the assignment, he responds with short, defensive answers.

Or perhaps you have a teenager that responds to your question of "How are you today, Honey?" with a short "Fine" and stays in her room for the rest of the night. How are the underlying moods of these beings affecting Your Own Universe?

Are you easily manipulated and pulled downward to their mood or are you powerful enough to pull them upward towards your "Green Zone" mood – assuming that you are in a Green Zone mood? What happens when you are in the Red Zone and they respond in the same ways? The store clerk might find herself embarrassed at the loud scene you create when you tell her to "Find somewhere else to work if you hate your job that much!" The co-worker could find himself in the boss's office explaining why he is the cause of your failure on the project. And the teenager – well, she can just forget about using your car over the weekend.

What does Your Own Universe look like now?

> *The more accurately*
> *one is able to pinpoint their "real" mood,*
> *the more power one has*
> *over managing it to get the result they desire.*

Mood ZONES

In order to understand how mood is the determining factor in the results YOU get, it is necessary to understand the zones in which various moods are classified.

In his book *The Secrets to Increasing Your Power, Wealth and Happiness*, Alan Walter describes "The Zones" as Red, Yellow and Green Zones, to define the various levels in which a person can live and/or perform according to their corresponding mood levels. Robert S. Kaplan, Baker Foundation Professor at Harvard Business School and former Dean of the Tepper School of Business at Carnegie Mellon University, along with his co-creator David

P. Norton, created the well known 'Balanced Scorecard' method which has been endorsed by corporate heavyweights such as Mobil and Sears. The method uses Red, Yellow, and Green zones to link a company's current actions to its long-term goals providing executives with data upon which they may make decisions and develop strategies.

The iMAGE Wealth Management system uses these same Zone classifications to help the student classify various moods and the energy levels they encompass. This makes recognizing various moods and their influence on iMAGE quick and easy.

RED ZONE iMAGE Characteristics:

- Low self-esteem (sometimes masked with over-confidence)
- Dangerous or harmful to themselves or others
- Acts/Reacts with distrust, dishonesty, confusion, prejudice, and negativity
- Blames others for their problems and failures
- Often experiences poverty

When operating for prolonged periods in the Red Zone, individuals often have poor timing, attract the "wrong" people in their lives and experience many failures.

They tend to have poor "soft skills", such as communication and the ability to handle people. They have a tendency to work against others rather than with others, and are resistant to change. They often *impair* or *demolish* others and situations, fail to take risks, and are often stuck in the past while reliving past hurts.

YELLOW ZONE iMAGE Characteristics:

- Low self-esteem in certain areas and confidence in others
- Hopeful and generally productive
- Acts/Reacts with criticism

- Prefers the status quo
- Dislikes instability

People who are experiencing Yellow Zone moods often feel moderately energized but move very slowly through space and time, operating mostly from habit.

When operating for prolonged periods in the Yellow Zone, individuals often have satisfactory timing. They do fairly well at handling things, places and subjects, but tend to struggle with communication and people-handling skills.

They usually work for others and are ambivalent when making decisions. They can be resistant to change but can be coaxed through their resistance. They often *impair* others and situations, can be encouraged to take risks, and sometimes dwell on past hurts.

GREEN ZONE iMAGE Characteristics:

- High self-esteem
- Confidence
- Dependability
- High ethical standards
- Optimism
- Extreme intelligence

People who are experiencing Green Zone moods often feel highly energized and move very swiftly and gracefully through space and time. When operating for prolonged periods in the Green Zone, individuals often have perfect timing and are in the right place at the right time and attract the right people in their lives.

They tend to have outstanding communication and people handling skills. They are readily found in positions of leadership and work with others rather than against them. They are confident making decisions and often take risks. They embrace change and can be led when necessary. They make more of others and situations and spend the majority of their time in the present.

It is important to know that it is a normal human function to experience Red, Yellow and Green Zone moods. However, our society often discourages us, at a very young age, from feeling and/or expressing Red and Yellow Zone moods. Remarks like "Big boys don't cry"; "Stop acting like a child"; and "Everybody loves a winner. No one wants to be around a looser"; all teach us that any moods other than Green Zone moods are unacceptable. Rather than to allow ourselves to acknowledge and experience the unwanted moods, we deny and suppress them. It is no wonder that after 30 or 40 years of doing this, many of us find ourselves with more hang-ups than a telemarketer. The next time you experience anger, self-pity, boredom or any mood other than a winning, friendly, Green Zone mood, try the following two mood management techniques.

Mood Time Management technique:

1. Identify your mood: "The mood I am experiencing is _____".
2. Depending on the downward level of your mood, set a timer or stop watch for 30 minutes. NOTE: It may be necessary to set a time limit of 1 – 2 hours in extreme cases. But do not go longer than 48 hours.
3. Find a private and safe space. If you are at work, perhaps you can go to your car.
4. In the allotted time, allow yourself to fully experience and express your mood.

If you feel the need to cry, yell, and scream, do so. If you feel the need to be more physical, i.e. pound on something, roll up a newspaper and pound it on a hard, non-breakable surface. In most cases you will not need to go more than 30 minutes. Try to feel the feeling for at least 30 minutes anyway. You will probably experience that the mood "runs out" in 15-20 minutes. You will be amazed at your mood when it does run out. I guarantee that YOU will have a higher mood level than when you began the process.

I-ACE Mood Management technique:

1. **Identify the mood:** The mood I am experiencing is _____.

2. **Acknowledge the mood:** I acknowledge that _____ is a temporary mood.

3. **Concentrate fully on the mood** by asking yourself the following questions:

    a. What do I believe to be true about feeling _____ (mood)?

    b. What do I like about feeling _____?

    c. What do I agree with about feeling _____?

    d. What am I willing to accept about feeling _____?

    e. What am I willing to do about feeling _____?

    f. What responsibility am I willing to own about feeling _____?

4. **Elevate the mood by identifying its opposite (antonym).**

    a. What is the opposite of _____ (original red or yellow zone mood)?

    b. Describe a time that I experienced (the green zone opposite mood). *List as many details as possible, who, what, when, where, how.*

    _____
    _____
    _____

    c. What do I believe to be true about _____ (the green zone opposite mood)?

    d. What do I agree with about feeling _____?

    e. What responsibility am I willing to own about feeling _____?

When YOU can manage your mood during challenging times, the mind has more energy to run its process of providing solutions and YOU will have more power to choose the best solution. The body will have the energy to carry out the necessary actions resulting in a win, even in challenging times. The more honest you are, the greater your results. Now identify your mood. YOU should have experienced a shift upward from the original red or yellow mood. If you still are not feeling green zone, repeat the I-ACE technique until you do.

***Remember that YOU have the power
to manage your mood and not the reverse.***
*You can change your mood
at any moment YOU so choose
if you're willing to be honest
about what you are feeling.*

I strongly recommend that anyone who is serious about mood management begin to study various moods using a dictionary. Begin with those moods that are most familiar to you no matter how basic. Research each mood and its antonym.

MOOD ZONE CHART

The following chart can be useful in identifying your mood. The first column is a section of our Process Maturity Chart™ *, used by our more advanced iWM students who are striving to attain mastery of their moods and skills. *

The forth and fifth columns are **Yellow Zone** moods which trend downward towards **Red Zone** moods. This downward trend usually ends with a person becoming totally absent and a sense of disconnectedness.

The second and third columns are **Green Zone** moods/antonyms that trend upward in energy level.

To effectively use the chart, locate your downward mood level in columns four and five using a dictionary to insure accuracy. If the mood chosen is in column four, its antonym will be located directly across from it in column two. Likewise columns three and five correspond.

Once the mood is identified, begin running the I-ACE technique. Remember, sincerity and honesty is most important when self-processing.

---

* The PMC is the trademark of Jordan P. Whitfield – process improvement specialist, Six Sigma Black Belt.

iMAGE is POWER

Stages	Green Zone		Yellow Zone	
Next Growth	Ambitious	Passionate	Apathetic	Dull
Correction	Dynamic	Purposeful	Complaisant	Shrunken
	Animated	Jovial	Subdued	Serious
	Playful	Lively	Restrained	Stifled
Effective Power	Efficient	Certain	Ineffective	Unsure
	Confident	Bold	Insecure	Unassertive
	Creative	Ecstatic	Shallow	Sober
	Elation	Thrilled	Disheartened	Disenchanted
	Enthusiastic	Excited	Indifferent	Bored
	Exuberant	Optimistic	Dispirited	Pessimistic
Enhance Quality	Mildly Optimistic	Attentive	Skeptical	Neglected
	Focused	Observant	Uninterested	Unobservant
Production	Cheerful	Harmonious	Dreary	Tense
	Friendly	Appreciated	Angry	Resentful
Establish Position	Encouraged	Peaceful	Discouraged	Disturbed
	Fearless	Reassured	Fearful	Scared
	Satisfied	Relieved	Discontented	Distressed
	Glad	Driven	Sad	Idle
	Victorious	Successful	Victimized	Failure
Planning	Principled	Accountable	Self-pity	Guilt
	Dignified	Worthy	Ashamed	Humiliated
	Proud	Blessed	Remorseful	Sorrowful
	Independent	In Control	Dominated	Manipulated
	Embraced	Persistent	Avoidance	Surrender
	Ambitious	Sentient	Despair	Numb
	Helpful	Forgiving	Abused	Revengeful
	Trusting	Respectful	Distrusting	Sarcastic
	Convicted	Secure	Martyr	Suffering
	Reliable	Faithful	Unreliable	Betrayed
Introduction	Modest	Organized	Self-righteous	Chaotic
	Composed	Centered	Hysterical	Unbalanced
	Attached	Open	Detached	Closed
	Present	Connected	Absent	Disconnected
Not Started	Green Zone		Red Zone	

Red   Yellow   Green

The important thing to understand is that *YOU are not your mood*. YOU are bigger than your mood if you choose to be. How do you know the difference? Use the Emotional Phrasing technique.

Emotional Phrasing technique

Choose a phrase that has some of your attention tied up in it or has a charge (strong feeling somewhere in your body) when you say it. Let's use, *"What if they criticize me?"* as an example. While being as authentic as YOU can, repeat the phrase using the following mood levels. Repeat the phrase 2 times in each mood level:

Happily:	*"What if they criticize me?"*
Jokingly:	*"What if they criticize me?"*
Sadly:	*"What if they criticize me?"*
Fearfully:	*"What if they criticize me?"*
Angrily:	*"What if they criticize me?"*
Relieved:	*"What if they criticize me?"*
Lovingly:	*"What if they criticize me?"*
Sexy:	*"What if they criticize me?"*
Nonchalantly:	*"What if they criticize me?"*
Winningly (as if YOU just crossed the finish line of a 10K race):	*"What if they criticize me?"*

How did you do? Of course this exercise is much more effective when it is being led by a facilitator who can detect if you are being authentic or if YOU are capable of showing even more emotion. It is also more challenging to do in front of a group. Consider trying it with friends, family and co-workers.

You probably experienced that some moods were more difficult to express than others. If so, that is your indication that the mood is bigger than YOU and that there is work to do in that area to release energy and emotions that are trapped by that mood. If you had absolutely no problem with this exercise and you were alone while doing it, I strongly suggest that you try it in front of someone else or a group of others. If YOU are still able to be authentic in your mood expression, then head to your nearest performing arts theater and audition for the leading role in their next production. There is a reason why movie stars like Angela Basset, Julia Roberts, Morgan Freeman, Tom Cruise, Sean Connery and a host of others, are paid so much for their performances; they are Masters at Mood Management and if you practice the drills in this book YOU will be on your way to becoming one also.

There are numerous benefits to mastering mood management other than becoming a star on the big screen. Making decisions under pressure and keeping a cool head becomes easier. A Mood Management Master – MMM – can also accept criticism from others without internalizing their emotions and reacting to what is being said. They also have the ability to manage the red and/or yellow zone emotions often accompanied with criticism, while refraining from judging themselves and those who criticized them. This makes it easier for them to discern if the information has usefulness in their overall improvement.

Can you imagine how powerful one must be to allow their emotions to simply wash over them while listening and being fully present with the information that is being given to them, and then, at will, going back and experiencing, duplicating, permeating and releasing those emotions? This skill can be so powerful when dealing with children, spouses, co-workers, partners, customers, vendors, relatives and oppositionists.

I realized that I was becoming a MMM when I was asked to present iMAGE Wealth Management to a group of high powered executives at an Innovation Forum. I had managed to calm my body's auto-response to presenting a new idea to a group of my peers. I was about 5 minutes into the presentation and feeling powerful! I asked the group to pair up because I was about to lead them through a presence drill. To my surprise, one of the participants, in a **very** loud, yellow zone voice, asked, *"Excuse me but why are you presenting this information? I thought we were here to discuss innovation. And what does this drill have to do with how we are going to make this city a leader in attracting innovative companies?"*

In microseconds, blood rushed from my feet to my head. I could feel my ears turn red with fire. I felt a downward pull on my spirit. My heart started pounding so hard it was drowning out my thoughts. My mind went into protective mode and started flashing me pictures and solutions on how to deal with the man and handle this situation. With what seemed like hundreds of pictures, strategies and moods flashing in front of me at once, I latched onto an image of me jumping across the table in my white dress and black heels, using my martial arts techniques to incapacitate him. I pictured myself pulling him from his seat, and holding him down with my foot pressing his head to the floor as I say: ***"Never interrupt the Zen Princess when she is speaking!"***

Suddenly, I felt a jolt to my temples and a voice said, "NO! Demonstrate!" Thrust back into the present, I took a breath from my abdomen and exhaled through my nose. Then I pictured my 75-year old father on his motorcycle, smiled and began to speak – slowly: *"I apologize if the material and exercises are causing you some discomfort. In the spirit of innovation, I am attempting to demonstrate an innovative way of managing ones' moods even during challenging times. I feel this information and these techniques will be useful to the group as we work together on finding creative ways to make our city more attractive to innovators; especially since we have diverse backgrounds and ideas which can sometimes cause tension in newly formed groups."*

The timing couldn't have been better because I had just finished explaining the zones in which people find themselves. I couldn't have asked for a better example of a red zone, "work against others" behavior.

The head of the forum stepped in and further explained why he thought iMAGE Wealth Management would be an exciting and innovative way to start the meeting. The gentleman (although I hesitate to call him that) calmed down and actually participated in the drills. I cannot say how much the drills benefited him, but the fact that he willingly participated in them told me that the technology was working on some level. Often, it is not until later that people actually realize the benefits of iWM.

Thank the "goodness" (the part that lives inside me) that I chose the course I did. After the class, another participant came up to me and remarked at how impressed she was at how I was able to "hold my space" and not let him "pull me down to his level". She said that whatever tool I used to do that, she needed it. Several weeks later, she became a client/student and is now well on her way to becoming a MMM.

So, how badly do YOU want *authentic* mood management, not an outward Green Zone mood with an underlying Yellow or Red Zone mood that others can detect even if they cannot precisely identify it? How badly do YOU want to be able to enjoy your life even in the midst of uncontrollable circumstances? How badly do YOU want to attract other Green Zoners who are winning at their games and want to help YOU win at yours? Practice, presence and patience are the key! But you might want to look the word patience up in your dictionary before you decide.

Moods

Thoughts . . .

iMAGE is POWER

Definitions . . .

GAMES ▸▸▸

In order to play any game and get effective results, one must know their abilities vs. skills vs. mastery. The process of accurately identifying the difference requires honesty and often an outside observer to help. When it comes to mapping out games and roles, these distinctions can determine how the game needs to be played to produce a win.

> ***Ability*** *can be defined as the innate aptitude and power to do; the capacity to achieve; talent*

It would be pointless to apply for a position as an administrative assistant if you cannot type. What kind of iMAGE would you project if you were asked to type correspondence for your manager and she emerged from her office to find you searching for the letters on your keyboard while pecking with two fingers? I'd be surprised if she remained in a green zone mood after seeing that.

> ***Skill*** *can be defined as a refined ability.*

There is a difference between ability and skill. For example, most human beings are born with the ability to walk. The average process that humans experience refining our walking ability into a skill is as follows: first crawling, then holding onto objects and pulling up while balancing, and then taking steps while holding onto the object. Over time, and with practice, we develop the ability to walk into a refined ability, or a skill. With years of practice, we elevate our level of skill into mastery. Many of us can actually chew gum and walk simultaneously.

> ***Mastery*** *can be defined as having full power and control over a subject or area that can be demonstrated by consistently producing results of excellent quality.*

Once you can differentiate between your abilities, skills and areas of mastery, you can then begin to align yourself with the game(s) you want to play. Once you understand what is required to play the game, you can assess which of your abilities may need to be refined to skills and which skills may need elevating to mastery to achieve winning results in the game. For example, perhaps you are a member of a civic organization and would like to play the game of chairman. After assessing your abilities, you realize that you have the skill to recruit new members and mastery of leadership. However, you have only an ability to fundraise, which is a major requirement for the position. A perfect alternative is to play the game of vice-chair or co-chair, which allows you to play at your current ability/skill level while developing your fundraising skill, positioning you to be the future chair of the organization.

If you are playing the right game for YOU, you will continue to be challenged, driving you to refine your abilities into skills. The important thing to know is that you can be a Green zone person yet have a Red Zone experience when developing a new skill and/or playing a new game. This does not make YOU a Red Zoner. Simply put, you progress from a place that is unknown, or unfamiliar, up the mood scale until you reach the Green Zone to end at abundance, power, empowerment or mastery. Once you embrace the process of mastery, you will welcome, rather than resist the process. Over time, you will become a master at your skill and/or game.

We are seldom a witness to the process that many masters go through before achieving mastery. Seeing only the end result, many of us are disillusioned with thoughts of achieving the same success without enduring the process of mastery. Tiger Woods presents a perfect example of the often hidden process of mastery. It almost seems that he appeared from nowhere and began beating everyone he played. There are those who don't even remember a time when he wasn't the face of golf. When Woods had to have reconstructive knee surgery in April 2009, it could have ended his career. Instead he was quoted as saying, *"The upside is that I have been through this* process *before and know how to handle it. I look forward to* working through *the rehabilitation* process *and getting back to action as quickly as I can."*

Woods was out of the spotlight for many months. He returned on February 23, 2009 to play at the Accenture Match Play championship, and lost. He played the CA Championships in Miami on March 9, 2009 and finished tied for ninth place. Then he played the Arnold Palmer Invitational March 29, 2009 and rolled in a birdie putt on the *final hole* to take the title.

Wow!! Talk about mood management; this guy knows the importance of maintaining a high mood level no matter what the situation. I suspect that he felt some sense of disappointment and frustration during and/or after those first two return games. However, he moved through those moods and up into what I refer to as "the Green Zone" – where our true power to affect outcome resides. Knowing his abilities and being willing to go through the process of refining his skills, gives Tiger Woods an image of mastery.

> ***Game*** *can be defined as any activity involving a skill in which there is a designated playing area, rules and regulations, liberties and limitations, fans, opponents, sometimes teammates, and a way of measuring success.*

In our society we tend to fluctuate in our use and acceptance of the word game. On one hand the word game is used as a negative: *"Don't play games with me – I need to know if you are telling me the truth!"* On the other hand, we use it often when we want to express our level of skill or capability: *"I need to up my game,"* or *"He's in the real estate game,"* or *"You better bring your "A" game."*

The concept of "game" is a key component in the iMAGE Wealth Management technology. In order to master any game, one must understand roles and identities.

> ***Role*** *can be defined as the proper or customary function, the rights, obligations, responsibilities, and expected behavior patterns associated with a particular position.*

The rules for the role do not change. They are the same for whoever is playing the role.

> ***Identity*** *can be defined as the personality one brings to the role.*

Let's say, for example, that the game is driving. The role would be driver. Every driver must have a driver's license and obey the same rules of the road. The identity is the *personality* of the driver. The driver could be the person that obeys all the rules and never goes over the speed limit, or the driver could be the maniac that honks at the vehicle in front, jumps from lane to lane trying to get ahead and speeds up at yellow lights only to be caught by the next red light. The identity determines how the role will be played through its code of ethics.

> ***Ethics*** *can be defined as the rules or standards governing the conduct [rightness or wrongness] of a person or the members of a profession.*

The identity decides what ethics will be used in all game play. Ethics are precepts (rules or beliefs that may or may not be the truth) that when applied in game play, determine results. There are "constructive" ethics and then there are "constrictive" ethics.

When examined closely, **Constructive Ethics** appear to have a "rightness" that would result in a win for everyone involved in the game.

For example:

1. I am committed to being fully present with the game.
2. I honor my spirit, mind and body.
3. I am honest.
4. I am truthful.
5. I am loyal to myself.
6. I honor my priorities.
7. I am committed to keeping my promises.
8. I am responsible for my actions.

iMAGE is POWER

Constrictive Ethics, on the other hand, may or may not create the ideal game environment for success.

For example:

1. You can't trust people.
2. Don't talk to strangers.
3. It's who you know not what you know. You have to know someone to get ahead.
4. Sometimes you <u>have</u> to lie; no one tells the truth 100% of the time.
5. You win some; you loose some.
6. Always look out for number one.
7. All you have is family.
8. All is fair in love and war.

Ethics will be discussed in greater detail in Chapter 8. Though ethics and morals could be the subject of endless debate, what is important for you to know is that YOU must review your ethics and decide if they are serving you well in the game or games you are playing.

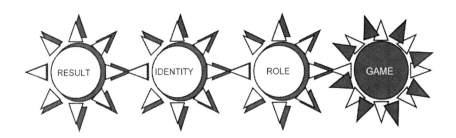

Diagram 1

This diagram graphically demonstrates that every result (desired and undesired) is attached to an identity that is responsible for manifesting that result. The identity is attached to a role and the role is attached to a game.

*If YOU are not getting the results you want,
map out the game and identify the breakdown
in the process that caused the results.*

Thoughts . . .

Definitions . . .

What games are you playing? ▶▶▶

Based on the principle that all the roles we play in life are attached to a specific game, it is easier to position yourself for success in the areas of your interest when you evaluate the situation without emotions. Using the definition of *game* as previously explained, mapping out the game you are playing, or want to play, becomes very simple when combined with a systematic approach.

The iMAGE Wealth Management method is called **Gameing**. In the **Gameing** method we use a Game Book to thoroughly view the game(s) we are playing, or want to play, without emotions or judgment.

> *Once your game is thoroughly mapped and viewed,*
> *YOU can decided how YOU feel about the game,*
> *and if YOU are playing the right game*
> *or if it is time to play a new game.*

How will you know if you are playing the right game, in the right position; or if you understand all the rules of the game and have the proper skill level to win? Are you taking full advantage of the liberties/freedoms of the game and respecting the limitations/barriers? Are you aware of who is on your side and rooting for your victory or who is waiting for you to show agony in defeat? The Gameing Method forces the player to look at their vision of the win. If YOU don't know what a WIN looks like, how can you play to win?

The key to winning any game is to study and understand the game; and as discussed earlier, studying is a skill. The more knowledge you have, the better your strategy. The better your strategy and the integrity of your practice, the greater your odds are at winning. Notice that nothing is being said about how you feel about the game. The idea is to map out your game and then decide how you feel about it and whether or not you want to play.

A professor teaching a public speaking course at a local university asked me to present the iWM Mood Management techniques to his students because they were extremely "fearful" of public speaking. I began the class with a review of Master Napoleon Hill's view on "The Six Basic Enemies" from his book *The Law of Success*. He explains that every fear can be categorized as one of the six enemies that keep us from "winning". They are:

Fear of Poverty   *Fear of Ill Health*

Fear of Criticism   *Fear of Old Age*

Fear of Loss of Love   *Fear of Death*

Next, I had the students define the word *fear*. They were surprised when I showed them the definition from Dictionary.com.: **noun 1.** a distressing emotion aroused by <u>impending</u> **danger, evil, pain**, etc., whether the threat is real or imagined; the feeling or condition of being afraid.

As they read the definition aloud, I noticed their physical manifestations in the form of frowns, stutters, smiles and an obvious "oh wow". These manifestations immediately told me that many of them were beginning to doubt that *fear* was actually what they were feeling about the game of public speaking. Agreeing that they were not in danger, they did not consider the audience or the game evil, and they did not associate pain with the game (unless, of course, their speech was to announce to a group of employees that they were no longer employed), they concluded that they were not in fear but more insecure or anxious about the game.

Now in a better mood about the game, they were ready to map out the public speaking game to move them towards a win. The first order of business was to change the name of the game. Since the "public speaking" game has a great deal of negative charge attached to it, I suggested that they change the name of the game to "Verbal Contribution". The next time YOU are asked to "give a speech, talk, or keynote address" change it to "I've been asked to give a verbal contribution on _____". Now doesn't that feel much better than public speaking?

Diagram 2, The Game Plan (page 63), illustrates the process I gave the class to map the "verbal contribution" game for a fictitious person whose intention was to play the game as their main source of income.

The first step in the Game Plan identifies the playground: local only, state wide, national, or international. Is it in a building or specific location? If so, what building, where, how big is the room, how many seats. In our example, the "contributor's" playground is a theater somewhere in the US and UK. It is important to list as many details about the playground as possible. This helps YOU, your mind, and body get present with your physical area of play and helps develop a holographic picture of the game in your mind.

Step 2 is to list the rules of the game and the skills required to win. Depending on the game, the rules can be quite numerous. In many cases, it requires study and observation skills to identify all of them. In football, there are so many rules even the commentators debate over some of them. I recommend learning the rules and developing the skills that are specific to the position you want to play. As you play, practice and move towards mastery in your position, you can then begin to learn the rules for other positions.

There is an important distinction here:
there is mastery of your position in the game
and then there is mastery of the game.
Each of these is a process.

Liberties and limitations in gameing is an area in which identities become more noticeable. Recall that the identity is the personality brought to the role in a game and that it is a key determinant in the results of the game. Unlike the rules of the game, which are usually clearly defined and the same for everyone in the role, liberties and limitations leave more room for interpretation or misinterpretation. It is also an area where ethics may influence the identity's actions. In our Game Plan example the contributor has the liberty of using props. If the audience is composed of high school children, the contributor may not want to use an actual gun or music with foul language as props when speaking to them on gang violence in schools. Liberties and limitations allow the identity to make the role unique and interesting.

What games are you playing?

Diagram 2: The Game Plan

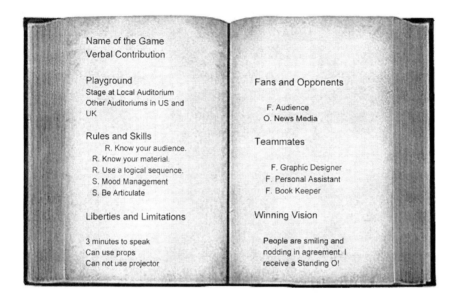

In gameing and in life, one always needs **fans**. The road to winning is arduous. Everyone needs a support system to win.

Opponents are a "dime a dozen"
but one fan can have the power and influence of 10 opponents.

If you don't have a fan, find one. If you aren't sure if they are a fan, ask them. If you have asked and can't identify one, take a long look at yourself. Perhaps you need to be a fan before you can appreciate having one. Either way, you must have someone cheering you on to navigate the laborious road to winning.

What about **teammates**? Well, if you live long enough, you quickly learn that all teammates are not necessarily fans. Sometimes mood and ethics can lead to jealousy, envy, control and destruction. Sometimes they start out as fans and become opponents as you begin to attain mastery. And sometimes, they are fans in one area and opponents in others. Either way, it is a better use of your time and energy to simply allow these people to be who they are. Identify them as opponents and quickly move away from the emotion surrounding it. My father always said, *"You can live with a snake as long as you know it is there."* I would much rather identify someone as an opponent than to mistakenly believe that he/she is a fan. Which teammate are you? That is the real question.

The final step in the Game Plan is to develop a **winning vision**. In many ways, this is the first step. If you cannot envision winning – in full 3D detail – how can you win? Well, I believe that you can win without a vision, but you may find yourself winning at the wrong game, ending up unfulfilled, spending more time and energy than you would like, and/or exhausted after the win. If YOU are clear on your vision and have a game plan, you will waste far less time and energy getting to your desired result.

Many people fail to get the results they want in life because they lack a clear vision.

Again, being honest with yourself is the first step towards achieving any goal. If you need help clarifying your vision, use the following Vision Clarity Technique.

Vision Clarity Technique

1. What do YOU perceive that you want or need? State it in a positive. *(I perceive that I want to give an outstanding "verbal contribution" to my audience.)*

   _____
   _____
   _____
   _____
   _____

2. Get the idea of having IT. Try to visualize it in detail.
   a. What will having IT do for YOU? *(I will feel more confident and it will help members of the audience avoid gang violence.)*

   _____
   _____
   _____
   _____
   _____

   b. What 3 things will you see? *(1. I will see me walking across the stage to the podium with confidence. 2. I will see the audience smiling and waiting for me to begin. 3. I will see them giving me a standing ovation.)*

   _____
   _____
   _____
   _____
   _____

c. What 3 things will you hear? *(1.I will hear them laughing at my stupid jokes. 2. I will hear the applause of the audience. 3. I will hear their comments on how I inspired them.)*

_____
_____
_____
_____
_____

d. What 3 things will you feel? *(1. I will feel extreme pride. 2. I will feel powerful. 3. I will feel relieved.)*

_____
_____
_____
_____
_____

3. When, where and with who do you want IT? *(In two weeks at the local high school with juniors and seniors present.)*

_____
_____
_____
_____

4. Are there any situations and circumstances in which you do not want it? *(I don't want IT if the principle and teachers do not buy in and support me.)*

What games are you playing?

5. How will getting it impact other parties – the pros and cons for family, friends, colleagues, customers, fans, opponents etc. *(My family will not see as much of me while I am preparing and may feel a sense of loss at first. My family will benefit from the financial gain as a result of my impact on the students. The students will be inspired to ask for help.)*

6. What internal and external resources do you have available to help you attain IT? *(Internally: I have great public speaking and acting skills. Externally: The principle is my younger sister so I will tell mom and dad about her drunken stupor when we were kids if she doesn't get on board.)*

iMAGE is POWER

7. How can you utilize the resources that you already have to attain IT? *(I will reuse the speech I prepared for another high school.)*

_____
_____
_____
_____
_____

8. Which of your fans want you to have IT? State their full name if possible. *(My sister, the teachers, the local police.)*

_____
_____
_____
_____
_____

   a. How do they support you in attaining IT? *(My sister will practice with me and offer suggestions based on her knowledge of the student audience.)*

_____
_____
_____
_____
_____

9. What are the first three steps YOU can take to achieve IT? *(1. Get my family's buy in. 2. Do research on gang violence in that school district. 3. Practice, practice, practice.)*

What games are you playing?

10. Affirm that YOU have IT. "I affirm that I have a clear vision of having_____ and I am grateful for the process of attaining IT". *(I affirm that I have a clear vision of having a powerful verbal contribution to the students and I am grateful for the process of attaining my powerful verbal contribution.)*

When you are entrenched in the process
of creating what you want,
and the road twist and turns,
and there are hail, snow and rain storms,
and fog so dense you can't see the forest or the trees,
cling to your vision and look for signs of spring.

iMAGE is POWER

Once you have mapped your game using the Game Plan, you are ready to outline the details of creation using the Player's Guide - Diagram 3. After restating the name of the game, it is important to set an intention for the game and then reaffirm the winning vision. When you are clear on your intention and can fully visualize the win, you are ready to map out the detailed steps using the Player's Guide as illustrated next.

Diagram 3: The Player's Guide

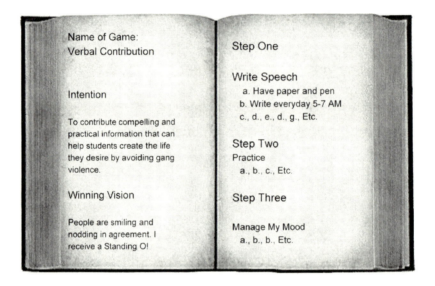

I am a firm believer in doing a "brain dump" and listing as many steps as possible initially. However, I have found in doing this exercise with numerous students that almost everyone has more favorable results when they concentrate their focus on only three steps at a time. Most find that those steps contain additional steps that need to be addressed. In truth, there is little value in constantly reviewing a long list of steps when one can only do a few at a time anyway. Breaking the list into small tasks creates a winning environment that will fuel YOU to continue the steps until you demonstrate your winning vision.

What games are you playing?

Use the sample Game Plan below to map out your game.

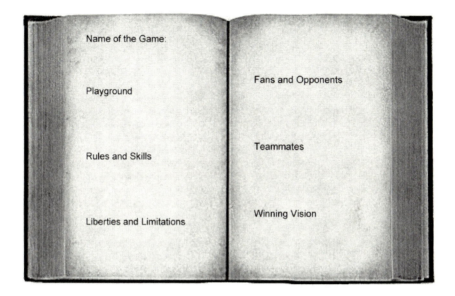

Notes:

_____
_____
_____
_____
_____
_____
_____
_____

iMAGE is POWER

Use the sample Player's Guide below to outline the details.

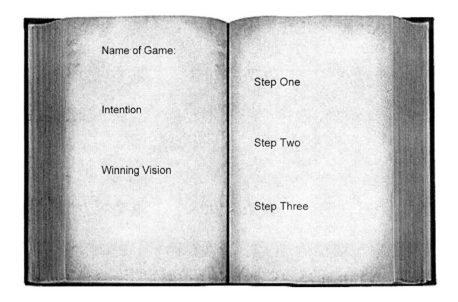

Notes:
_____
_____
_____
_____
_____
_____
_____
_____
_____

What games are you playing?

Thoughts . . .

iMAGE is POWER

Definitions . . .

Ethics ▸▸▸

First of all let me start by saying that I am no expert on ethics. There have been hundreds of books written on the subject and great debates over the difference between ethics and morals. The law defines what behaviors are legal and not, but the distinctions between "right" and "wrong" are not always clear. A being's belief system comprised of numerous experiences including parent's belief systems, religion, education, peer pressure, successes and failures, to name a few, is the foundation upon which ethics are created.

> ***Ethics*** *can be defined as a set of precepts that govern how YOU play the game.*
>
> ***Precepts*** *are rules or beliefs that are accepted as the truth but which may or may not be the truth.*

iMAGE is POWER

My belief on the subject of ethics as it relates to iMAGE Wealth Management is as follows:

- There are constructive and constrictive ethics.
- It is not my place to judge anyone else's choice of ethics. I can only attempt to live up to my own set of constructive ethical standards.
- One must "practice" living by their constructive ethics. We may have them but they may not always be easy to implement.
- Our code of ethics evolves as we evolve. Many of the decisions that I was comfortable making at 27 years of age, I would never make today. For example, when I was working for a corporation I had no problem showing up late for work, taking a two hour lunch, and leaving one hour early just because everyone else in the department had the same work ethic. Today, I usually begin work early, at the same time the birds awaken. I might work through lunch and as an entrepreneur, I never really stop working.
- Our ethics may change according to the game we are playing and who is playing with us. For example, if we are playing a game of chess with a 10-year old that is just learning the game, we might use a slightly revised set of ethics than if we are playing with a 35- year old whose own ethics drive them not only to win but to humiliate us in the process.
- Our mood influences our decision to uphold our code of ethics, which is why mood management is vital to achieving winning results. For an extreme example: if someone seriously hurts our loved one, we might throw out our code of ethics that tells us "never take revenge into our own hands." Without being conditioned to manage our mood and regain power over the situation, it is conceivable that we might easily become one of the "good guys" in jail today.

Ethics and morals are the subject of endless debate but what is important for you to know is this:
YOU have to review your ethics
and decide if they are serving you well in the game
or games you are playing.

And how do you know? If you are getting the results you want in life; if you are playing with people you enjoy and respect vs. cheaters, liars, and victimizers (after all, birds of a feather …); if people admire you for your positive, friendly, and empowering reputation and want to play with you; if you are able to play games that result in a "win-win"; and most importantly, if you appear to have a temporary loss and still feel good about the way you played the game, then your ethical standards are allowing you to be a winner. If, on the other hand, you win but you don't feel good about it, or you win but others don't see you as a winner, you might want to re-evaluate the ethics by which you play.

If you find yourself in an ethical dilemma ask yourself the following questions:

1. Am I being honest?
2. Am I playing with principles in the game?
3. Am I willing to be responsible for the outcome?
4. Will my actions build goodwill?
5. Will the people I admire most be pleased with my performance?

If you can answer "Yes" to each of these questions, it is likely that you are playing ethically.

"When all is said and the children are in bed,"
the way you play the game is totally up to YOU.

In a previous chapter, I discussed *constructive* versus *constrictive* ethics. Below is a more comprehensive list of *constructive* ethics. If you are in the process of reviewing your ethics, consider adding these to aid you in winning your games.

1. I am committed to being fully present with the game.
2. I honor my spirit, mind and body.
3. I am honest and truthful.
4. I honor my priorities.
5. I am committed to keeping my promises.
6. I am responsible for my actions.
7. I am sincere in describing my mood.
8. I am sincere in recognizing my own reality.
9. I am steadfast in my standards of excellence and craftsmanship.
10. I own my strength and power.
11. I own my accomplishments and never devalue them.
12. I honor and share my knowledge for the greatest good of others.
13. I make my own decisions with doing the greatest good for others in mind.
14. I stay connected to my family and friends.
15. I honor and support those that have helped me in the past and those that are helping me now.
16. I am committed to communicating effectively with others.
17. I am responsible for my past.
18. I repay my debts.
19. I am grateful for my wins.
20. I celebrate my wins.

The only thing I have left to say about ethics is the old cliché:

> *"It's not whether you win or lose,
> but how you play the game that counts."*

Ethics

"**Wealth** *is the ability to fully experience life."*
Henry David Thoreau

"In everyone's life, at some time,
our inner fire goes out.
It is then burst into flame
by an encounter with another human being.
We should all be thankful for those people
who rekindle the inner **spirit**."
Albert Schweitzer

*"The **body** is a perfect servant of the mind."*
Unknown

"Truth *is one forever absolute,
but opinion is truth filtered through the moods,
the blood, the disposition of the spectator."*
Wendell Phillips

iMAGE is POWER

Thoughts . . .

Definitions...

Conclusion

So there you have it! iMAGE Wealth Management; a technology, a system for creating a powerful self image [or business image] while in a high mood level, and positions you to attract other individuals that will help you create the wealth you desire and deserve.

I have lived this technology and demonstrated its power to help me effectively communicate and handle people with grace and ease regardless of their mood. I know that I have the skills to hold my own space regardless of the challenges that confront me. If I run into someone who is in the Red Zone and I am in the Green Zone, they will be pulled up to my level rather than bring me down to theirs.

As I stated at the beginning of the book, it is not easy and it does take practice. But what I am confident of is that it works! I am living proof. Not everyone will get it. Not everyone will study it. Not everyone will use it. But for those who do, the results will be remarkable. They will build an iMAGE that is Powerful and know how to use that power to create wins. These people will be easy to recognize. They will be the ones who are winning, friendly, in the right place at the right time with the right people. They will be the ones who are working with others rather than against them. They will be the ones playing with other Green Zoners and attracting the wealth they desire. Are you one of them?

Be Tolerant...

"If common sense was common, everyone would have it."

Mic Alexander

Peace on your journey

Acknowledgements

There are so many people to thank that it would take a separate book to include all of you. I believe that everyone I have met while on my journey has contributed in some way to the manifestation of this book. Perhaps you were a fan and perhaps an opponent; either way, your presence in my life helped shape the experiences that has led me to this point on the journey; and I thank you.

Of special mention are the following spiritual beings:

My Brother: Dr. Elmore Dean Alexander – sister in law, Diane – nephews, Brandon & Drew and niece, Erin; being family is not always the easiest roles in life but what a blessing it is to have the opportunity to experience it, especially with all of you. Thank you for your love.

My Close/Extended Family: Uncle Otis, Kurt & Cara, Lisa & new baby, LaToya, Aunt Rosie & Uncle Butch, Aunt Wendy, Aunt Pat, Uncle James, Uncle Jr. & Aunt Erie; thank you for supporting me and my mom and dad over the years.

My Friends: Danette "Dani", Yvette, James, Eron, Junius; you have always been there for me whenever I needed you. I will never forget your kindness and genuine support. I love you all.

My Team: Candice Caldwell – Electronic Marketing Coordinator, Charles Harrison – Bus. Development, Denise Lasley – Editor, Ken Munkens – PR Director, Martin Peterson – Marketing Director, Jordan Whitfield – Financial Manager/Processor; I am truly blessed to work with a group of professionals like all of you. Your belief in me as an entrepreneur and your unwavering support has made all of this possible. Thank You!

My Screeners: LaToya, Claudie, Aunt Nancy, Dad, and Mom; thanks for your sincere feedback in shaping this book for everyone to enjoy.

The following people have graciously served as MY PRIMARY TEACHERS. Some are family and friends yet their teachings have influenced and inspired me to believe in myself and iMAGE Wealth Management as a reality that can help "the masses" learn to enjoy their journeys under any circumstances. I am honored and grateful to be your student.

Ms. Marilyn Addison: It has been a blessing to have you in my life! Thank you for being willing to hold up that big ole mirror in front of me. I also thank you for sharing your gift of essential healing oils with me and their effect on mood. I know that *Spiritual Blends, LLC.* will bless many who seek your knowledge.

Mr. Robert Audrey: You have taught me the importance of laughter and family. Thank you for all of the tear and laughter filled conversations over the years. Your teachings about the "games of life" and how to "win" at them are priceless.

Mrs. Angelina Corbet: You are a constant inspiration to me and others. Thank you for the enlightening conversations around feminine energy and for writing *'The Little Pink Book of Feminine Leadership'*. Your book and your work around the Enneagram have been an inspiration to me in developing iWM. Girl, you are the bomb! I love you and Drude.

Aunt Robette Goodwin: You are the sister I never had. Thank you for loving me all of these years – even when I wasn't so lovable. Most of all, thank you for your confidentiality and emotional support. Your constant demonstration of how abilities and ethics influence positive results have helped shape those chapters in the book. You inspire me to be better.

Drs. Light and Brian Miller: Your Ayurvedic teachings have kept me healthy mentally and physically during an arduous journey. I keep your books *'Ayurveda & Aromatherapy'* and *'Ayurvedic Curative Cuisine for Everyone'* close by at all times. Your teachings have influenced my understanding of how a healthy body influences mood. I thank you for your genuine love and support over the years. Namaste'

Mr. David Nelson: You have taught me the power of processing and maintaining a high mood level while reaching for my goals. You are a master processor and I am grateful to have you on my journey.

Sifu Gary Stier: You have taught me the benefit of being disciplined in my practice. Watching and studying with you has been a true blessing.

Sifu Jordan Whitfield: I could write a novel about what your love, friendship and teachings have meant to me and the iWM system. Without your leadership, guidance and training, iWM would have remained a thought. Thank you for pushing me, processing me and never giving up on me. I love you...always.

Author Alan C. Walter: I feel blessed to have had the opportunity to study at the Advanced Coaching and Leadership Center. Practicing your processes and applying your concept of presence has provided me the support and confidence I needed to create iWM.

Thank you for your years of dedication and study. Your teachings and master works around leadership and human behavior are impressive and inspiring to all who choose to study and explore their own unlimited potential. Peace and blessings.

My Other Teachers: Nate Barber, Dr. Rev. Beckwith, Allison Browning, Cheryl Cox, Michael Cadle, Don Lomax, Liam McGee, Dr. Lee Monroe, Brian Simmons, Barbara Spradling, Bridgette VanKammen, Julia and Lizzy Whitfield, and all the Seniors at The Villages in Florida; your lessons have taught and continue to teach me to keep going and keep growing…

Thank You All!

In Memory Of:

Nana, Mother, Grand Dad, My Ronnie,
Uncle Sony, Uncle George, Aunt Cookie,
Charlene, Bill, Mr. Thayer…

Thanks for looking out for me from the other side.

About the Author

◀◀◀◀▶▶▶▶

Mic Alexander was born and raised in Buffalo, New York. She attended Indiana State and Georgia State Universities with a focus in business and finance. She received her Graduate Assistant Status from Dale Carnegie Training and Certification for Coaching and Processing from Advanced Coaching and Leadership Center.

By age 30, Mic had started, developed and sold her interest in three successful businesses in the catering, import clothing and custom jewelry markets. She moved to Charlotte, North Carolina to become the CEO of her family's commercial printing company. It was during her leadership role with then, Overflow Printing Incorporated that she honed her business skills and began focusing on the importance of image management in building wealth.

Mic is a highly successful entrepreneur who has attained mastery in business start up, business development, image development, image improvement, and mood management. She is highly skilled in change management, business transition, training, manufacturing, process improvement, and negotiations.

Today, as the founder of the iMAGE Wealth Management Technology, she travels around the country lecturing and consulting with individuals, professionals, and business owners to teach them how to utilize the iMAGE Wealth 'Mood Management' processes to overcome challenging times and create winning results.

Mic resides in Charlotte, North Carolina and in her down time enjoys dancing, golfing, playing pool, boating, riding her motorcycle and just relaxing to the sounds of jazz - preferably at a spa.

For more information about iMAGE Wealth Management go to www.imagewealth.com

Top Judgment Words
- Need To
- Have To
- Must
- Better
- Always
- Never
- Can't
- Should

CPSIA information can be obtained at www.ICGtesting.com
Printed in the USA
BVOW040959070213

312458BV00008B/2/P